The Land That Grew Me

Mab Jones

First published in Great Britain by Selcouth Station Press in April 2020
ISBN: 978-1-8380-2280-8

Cover art by Lewis Jenkins
Cover design by Haley Jenkins
Website:
Typeset and formatting by Haley Jenkins
www.selcouthstation.com
Twitter: @SelcouthStation
Facebook: @selcouthstation
Instagram: selcouthstation

The Mother at Home

Tonight | I want to drink | the moon | it hangs there | like a glass | of milk |
all cream and promise | sharp edges | swollen to curds |

Tonight | I'm sitting | in my small room | top of | the tower | top of | the world |
and though I may seem | matron-weighty | my thin bones are pricking | to dance |

The curtains | drape | like curious girls | their faded blooms| grow round once
more | lipstick swirls | of red , and | now the sofa swells and puffs | shining like a
lover's tongue |as outside | clouds blow dark —

My children have all | been time-ticked away | and my mantelpiece | toothed with
their | faces | Even the finger | that once held the | lens has | buried itself | under
time's dust | but —

Tonight I am | as certain | as sun | as fierce | as its hydrogen heart |
Tonight I am | as light | as a star | I twirl | shining bright | as an atom |

My arms | grow fire | my legs | spout flame | I jump to the sky, and | I blaze —

The Ladies of the Boathouse

Written at the Dylan Thomas Boathouse in Laugharne

The window at my back cracks
open like a mouth, into this place
where a poet once was, and
where these women now are.

The heart of the house, these days,
is its stomach – its scones which
warm our noses; its soups which
pepper the salty air with herbs.

China teeters neatly in this kitchen,
where cups and plates are washed
as clean as teeth.

The women with precision are
baking, boiling, serving,
washing up the dishes
in the soapy, crumbloved sink.

Their work is just to feed the rising
tide of visitors, each day
a swell of such that
fills the slabstoned back,

as they make jokes and Welsh cakes;

chit-chat and cafe lattes;

these ladies of the Boathouse who are

its floury, hob-cwtched heart.

My Small Kitchen

Now my small kitchen lists its demands:
saucepans; ladles; a rolling pin with palm-
warmed handles; a cauldron, but modern,
capable of heating litres. A cross-hatch of
instruments, the apparatus of affection:
spoons to stir the soup with; a knife to cleave
the butter, golden, from its dish. Silver forks
to fondle your lips, my friends, my lovers;
this small kitchen already slow-brimming
with the soup of friendship and passion.

Ah, but it's a need, now, to feed you;
to feed myself. The beautiful boy next door
and the old man from the house, neither
of whom I can talk to - let the food from
my small kitchen be a tongue between us.
A honey cake for our conversation; smooth
mushroom soup to ease our tender throats.
My hob throbbing into midnight, the rack
both fervent and fevered, easing speech
between us through dishes new and known.

Rhigos

"This is the land that grew me,"
she says, as we speed to the top
of the Rhigos, where wild daffs
wait like valets at the skirts
of the waiting mountain.

We park the car near its feet and
she sprints up, confident as a ram,
while I stumble, wool-footed, the wet
grass filling my daps with water that's
winter-cold. There are tides

swimming within these hills but
I, city-dweller, am not familiar
with their rhythm or their flow.
She disappears into cloud whilst I sit,
flopping on scree composed,

I discover, of crystal, coke, and
slate, stuff I could use to build,
heat, and decorate a house - but
not here, where only the land is,
plus the odd tree or sheep, flower

or woman; the earth spitting its minerals,

offering up, as we clamber down,

a cowbone the size of a vase.

Summer City

For Cardiff

Originally published as part of the Poetry Arcades Project

In my memory this city is always summer:
the museum dome a scoop of vanilla;
the brewery chimney a dancing figure;
the hum of Queen Street like childsong,
the shoppers hopscotching to buy.
Though I am old and the veins now
jump like skipping ropes in my hands,
my hip bones stiff and as delicate as
meringue; and though winter comes
again, again, to smother us in grey,
still the city sits golden in my recollection:
the river a holiday bangle; the bay
as blue as a Tip Top; the eyes
of the houses smiling down
beneath the thrown ball of the sun.

Barry Island

I'm riding the back of a banshee
to Barry, the screaming, buckling body
of the train pramfull and bustling,
passing the eyes of houses, the arms
of roads; weaving under wiring, the pylons
standing guard. It's summer and
Maggie Fach will be there, with all
her holiday children - under sunhat,
over sandclot, fielding armfuls of ice-cream
into all those unfathered mouths. The sea
will marathon closer, bringing broken glass
and shells. The seagulls will dare a dive
when the littlest plops her cone. The
Pingu bins are waiting and the donuts
are mouthing their o's. I'm on my way on this
ghost train, in sunglasses, a spectre; single
woman amidst the babies; non-toddlered,
not belonging. As the sand castles rise I'll
finish this poem, the hissing sea for a friend.

Six Bells

It wasn't a blast, our tour guide said,
like the ones you see in James Bond:

a sudden explosive POW and then
the bodies thrown back from the force,

no - it was more like an opening scene
from the film Mission Impossible,

where the fire neatly follows the fuse,
a strolling slick of flame. The men

would have seen it seconds before
a blazing, burning wall, which came

as if from nowhere, and shut their lungs
like mouths. Now, there is only silence, and

the blackbird's blossoming song, as we walk
along together on top of the closed-up mine.

Pendine

A man tells another man of a
different man who once broke the
world land speed record here.

But this is also where Molly
and Milly took their dog-child
for a walk, back when their love

was new but an old rule made it
outlaw. Tell me, which goes faster -
the forward hurl of civilisation, or

Cupid's haphazard arrow?
Tell me, which is greater -
the passion of man's competition

with man, or that
                    of two women's embrace?

Again, I Think Of Moving

Written sat by a seaside slip road in Criccieth

But what would I do, up here in the north,

where the sea is blue and moaning,

and all the hunched-up castles

remind me of defeat?

What would I do, in this titchy village,

with little besides a butcher, baker,

Bargain Booze, except eat bloody

sausages, too many currant buns,

grow fat and alcoholic, and still always

think about you?

Slip roads are made for slipping, cariad,

and waves for postcards or drowning.

The north wasn't made for women like me

who can't drive, or swim, or forget.

Cardigan

So named, she thought, for a once-Wales
where people coddled their limbs in knitted
things roped together by the cabled hands
of women, their tongues and needles clicking
as the men went out to hunt and shear
the silvered fish and blossoming lambs,
beneath the bosomy hills, and over a sense
of history as sure as the ribboning river.

Now a supermarket shines too-bright near
the town, where rooftop aerials spear the ether,
cut crackling holes in her cloudy sense of what
was. The women knitting their brows as the men
click remote controls, screens glowing renditions
of a past both true and not-true; overly splendid
but simple; a woolly perception she cradles
as her cranium plain-stitches the name.

Cupboard

I, who've inherited nothing, except
this nose more arched than a harp,
these bones made to cradle a life,
find in these old things enough
to still my quivering beak, which
pricks in every direction of a map;
enough to soothe the soup of my belly,
which craves to feed to lips of a babe.

Be still. These delicate, finely-wrought
treasures sit in a cupboard that's cradle-
sized. My eyes sip at them daily,
when making tea, slipping the coats
from potatoes. Two cruets, as white as
atoms; twin egg cups, as blue as forever.
The bowls I bought back in Kyoto,
black and red, lacquered like beads.

A glass patterned with the queen
of hearts, fashioned by hand in the
50s. An iron teapot, for ceremonies
by kimono-clad women, or samurai.
Is there a difference? I twirl my knife
and hum, keep my pattern of daily
ritual before these sitting things,

their bodies as sturdy as Buddhas.

Cleared from the homes of the dead,

they are small joys which, in my

small world, loom large. The dust

which rests on them, settles me.

Relics and remnants, shy souvenirs; yet

their presence calms as I cut carrots,

slice bread, my bird nose still for a minute,

my stomach quiet for a time.

Valli Takes a Bath

Written whilst at Skanda Vale, Llanpumsaint

I step through a hatch of shadow and we're

nose to trunk, my white eye drawn up to that one

which is liquid as amber, brown as a coconut,

tufted lashes thick as the brush the monk uses

to soap the creature clean. Valli

is two years younger than I am, but

her wrinkles are rivulets to let the water run,

to hold the mud her dermis needs to breathe.

She was born as my hands, my face, will become:

lined and creased, parchment pressed into shape

around the cosmic dust of bones. I watch as she dips

the soft lips of her trunk into the metal bowl

and blasts her body with suds. Brother

bathes her twice a week, he says, sloughing

the flesh from her hulk so it can replenish,

the fresh skin a regeneration which, in this

land, requires man's hand in the place of palms.

My own show paths fanning into futures I won't know as

the frayed map edge of her ears gently furl,

the mala beads of her forehead shine. Her strength and her

tenderness are as everyday and as unstoppable

as time; as humble and as powerful as a birth.

She is a firebreath of life wrapped in a dinosaur form,

natal yet ancient, primordial but still in the hands

of the priest as, during our end, that great cleansing, we all are.

Other Titles by Selcouth Station Press:

Our Voices in the Chaos by David Lewis (2019)

And If I Die Tomorrow by Willem Myra (2019)

Become Something Frail by Stuart Buck (2019)

The Living Museum by Edward Garvey-Long (2019)

Death's Daughter by Fanni Suto (2019)

Pretty to Think So by Samantha Edmonds (2019)

My Father, from a Distance by Scott Manley Hadley (2019)

Just Let Me Have This by Heather Sweeney (2018)

Conversations with Dad by Jacqueline Robinson (2018)

Henry's Departure by K.D. Rye (2018)